Percival,
the Performing Pig

A One Act Play by Dilys Owen

Samuel French - London
New York - Toronto - Hollywood

CHARACTERS

STAGE MANAGER	LORRY DRIVER
PRODUCER	HIS MATE
SCARECROW	HOTEL MANAGER
PERCIVAL	LORD POSH
GRANDFATHER TURKEY	LADY POSH
A HEN	THEATRE MANAGER
HIRAM J. POTTER	DOCTOR WHEEZUM
OLD MACDONALD (the farmer)	DOCTOR SNEEZUM
A SMALL TURKEY	DOCTOR TONIC
ANIMALS	
THE SCENERY	

SCENE: A stage.

TIME: The present.

PRODUCTION NOTE

Apart from the animals, and unless indicated, most of the cast wear
ordinary clothes, with characterization suggested by details - cloth caps
for the Lorry Driver and his Mate, etc.
The animals could wear masks, but it would be better if the effect of
beaks, snouts, etc., could be suggested in their make-up, leaving facial
expressions visible.
Some of the smaller parts can be doubled.
The Stage Manager, Producer and Scarecrow, should be slightly older than
the others.
The play is performed in a plain curtain set.

PERCIVAL, THE PERFORMING PIG*

Opening music is a lively version of 'Old Macdonald had a farm', which is
faded out as the curtain rises. When the curtain goes up, three figures are
on the stage - the STAGE MANAGER, the PRODUCER and the SCARECROW -
all in earnest discussion, with their backs to AUDIENCE.

STAGE M.   But I tell you, the scenery isn't ready. How can we
                    possibly perform the play without any scenery?

SCARECROW   We've got to do something. Out there, hundreds of
                    people are waiting - we can't let them down.
                    We'll have to manage without scenery.

STAGE M.   )
PRODUCER   )   (in horror)   Without scenery?

STAGE M.   Oh, when I think of that wonderful farmhouse we
                    were going to have, with the pigsties and the
                    cowhouses and the weeping willow tree - . And
                    then the wonderful theatre for when we come to the
                    theatre scene, with a great chandelier, all shining -
                    oh, it's enough to break your heart, it really is.

SCARECROW   (noticing AUDIENCE)   Shhh! They're watching!

                    (They go into a huddle.)

PRODUCER   Whatever are we going to do?

SCARECROW
: We'll tell them about our difficulty. They look quite friendly, really - for an audience.

STAGE M.
: What do you think, Mr Producer?

PRODUCER
: Well, all right, but if they start throwing rotten tomatoes, I'm off.

SCARECROW
: (stepping forward importantly)   Ladies and gentlemen. Welcome to our play. This is the Producer - this is the Stage Manager.

(They bow.)

I'm the narrator. In case you hadn't noticed, I'm a scarecrow. That's because the first part of the play is set in a farmyard.

STAGE M.
: (in a piercing whisper)   Tell them about the scenery.

SCARECROW
: Oh yes. We were going to have wonderful scenery. Over there -   (As he speaks, he indicates various parts of the stage and sets the scene, becoming carried away and very friendly towards the AUDIENCE.)   - is the farmhouse. That's where Old Macdonald, the farmer, lives. It's got a lovely red roof, and ivy growing up the walls -

STAGE M.
: (shaking his head)   Oh, it was a beautiful farmhouse.

SCARECROW
: Now over here, are the pigsties. Oh yes, we have to have pigsties, because that's where Percival lives. Percival, the Performing Pig, the hero of the play -

PRODUCER
: (interrupting)   Get on with it. The scenery.

SCARECROW
: Oh yes. Well, right in the middle of the stage, here, we were going to have a great big weeping willow tree -

STAGE M.
: (nearly in tears)   Oh, it was such a beautiful tree.

PRODUCER
: What he means, ladies and gentlemen, is that the scenery's not ready, so we're going to do the play without it.

SCARECROW   (suddenly forgetting AUDIENCE)   Hey, I've got
                   an idea. Why don't we have live scenery?
                   (Turns to AUDIENCE again.)   That'll be better
                   than nothing, won't it?   (To the ACTORS in the
                   wings.)   Hey, you lot, come here a minute.

                   (Three children, dressed in ordinary clothes, enter.
                   They are SCENERY 1, SCENERY 2 and SCENERY 3.)

                   (arranging them round the stage)   If you two put
                   your hands on each other's shoulders, like that –
                   there's the farmhouse. And if you stand here, in the
                   middle of the stage – the weeping willow tree.

                   (The SCENERY hold these poses throughout the
                   following, staring stiffly straight into the AUDIENCE.
                   SCENERY 1 and SCENERY 3 are the farmhouse,
                   SCENERY 2 is the tree.)

                   There.   (To AUDIENCE.)   Of course, you
                   have to use your imagination as well. You'll have
                   to imagine the farmhouse and the willow tree. These
                   (Gestures over shoulder.)   are just to help you.

STAGE M.   (sadly)   And what we're going to do when we
                   get to the theatre scene, I really don't know.

SCARECROW   Are we all ready now? I think we can start. What
                   do you say, Mr Producer?

PRODUCER   (shouting)   Actors on stage.

STAGE M.   (shaking head as he goes off)   Oh, all that
                   beautiful scenery.

                   (Enter, in a line, PERCIVAL, GRANDFATHER
                   TURKEY, a HEN, a SMALL TURKEY and any number
                   of assorted ANIMALS. They go to their places in a
                   group to one side of the stage, and form a tableau,
                   which they hold while the SCARECROW speaks.)

PRODUCER   Over to you, Scarecrow.   (He goes off.)

SCARECROW   (coming D.S., where he takes up a position on the
                   opposite side to the ANIMALS)   There was
                   once a pig called Percival. He looked just the
                   same as any other sort of pig – but there was one

great difference. Percival had a beautiful voice.

(The ANIMALS mime a sequence where PERCIVAL sings, hand on heart, to the others, and they listen, as the SCARECROW speaks on.)

(telling the story with great emphasis)   He used to sit in the pigsty with his brothers and sisters, and sing to them. All the other animals would listen while he sang solos from famous operas, and at the end –   (He turns to watch the action.)

(The ANIMALS suddenly stop miming, and really make a noise.)

ANIMALS
(applauding loudly)   Hooray! Wonderful! Marvellous! What a voice!

A HEN
Hooray for Percival! Oh, what a wonderful singer he is!

GRANDFATHER T.
(singing, while beating time with a claw)   'For he's a jolly good fellow, for he's a jolly good fellow,   (The others join in.)   for he's a jolly good fellow, and so say all of us.'

(They sing right through to the end, and then clap and applaud, while PERCIVAL raises his hand and makes efforts to stop the noise.)

PERCIVAL
Please, dear friends. Please. Really, there's nothing so special about me –

(HIRAM J. POTTER enters suddenly, and interrupts from the side of the stage. He wears an overcoat, dark glasses, and waves a large cigar.)

HIRAM
Oh yes there is.

(Whispers of 'Who's that? Who can he be?' as the ANIMALS look to see who has spoken.)

(coming forward)   Allow me to introduce myself – Hiram J. Potter at your service. How lucky that my car broke down near your farm, otherwise I would never have stopped here – and never heard the wonderful voice of this very talented pig.
(Comes over to PERCIVAL, and shakes his hand.)

	Allow me to congratulate you, sir. Your future in opera is assured.
PERCIVAL	What does that mean?
HIRAM	Why, my dear sir, with a voice like yours, do you think I would allow you to remain here on a farm? No! You must come with me to London and sing on the stage, so that the world may hear what a wonderful voice you have. You'll be a sensation.
ANIMALS	(speaking at once) Oh no. We don't want you to go to London. Stay here with us, Percival. Don't leave us.
PERCIVAL	(when the noise has died down) I'm sorry, Mr Potter. I don't want to go to London, or sing on the stage. I like living here on the farm.
	(HIRAM looks determined, the ANIMALS anxious, as the SCARECROW takes up the tale.)
SCARECROW	But Mr Potter wouldn't listen. He made arrangements at once to buy Percival.
	(HIRAM goes across the stage to the 'farm', where he mimes a knock at the door, and OLD MACDONALD comes out.)
HIRAM	Now then, sir, I want to buy your pig.
OLD M.	(stroking chin) Well, I dunno. Percival's always been a satisfactory pig, as you might say. No trouble with him, like. I dunno as I want to sell him.
HIRAM	Oh, come sir. I'll give you a good price. (Takes out his wallet.)
OLD M.	Well now, that's a different matter –
HIRAM	(pressing money into his hand) It's a deal. I'll send a lorry tomorrow to collect him. (He goes out, looking very pleased.)
	(OLD MACDONALD looks at the money, nods approvingly, and goes back into the 'farm'. The ANIMALS have been watching this silently. They now burst out in indignant chorus.)

GRANDFATHER T.   It's a diabolical liberty. That's what it is.

A HEN   (tearfully)   Oh Percival, whatever will we do without you?

SMALL TURKEY   Who will sing to us?

SEVERAL ANIMALS   Yes, who'll sing to us if they take you away?

PERCIVAL   (lifting his hand for silence)   My friends, it'll be just as hard for me. I don't want to go to London, or sing on the stage. But what can I do?

GRANDFATHER T.   A plan of action, that's what we need. Think, all of you, think!

(All fall into attitudes of thought. The SCARECROW takes up the tale again.)

SCARECROW   So they thought and thought. A plan to save Percival. How could it be done? Then at last –

(GRANDFATHER TURKEY holds up a finger.)

GRANDFATHER T.   Ah! I've got it.

(The ANIMALS cluster round.)

ANIMALS   (overlapping)   What, Grandfather Turkey? Tell us.

(GRANDFATHER TURKEY mimes telling his plan, while the ANIMALS cluster round, miming excitement, approval and laughter. PERCIVAL shakes GRANDFATHER TURKEY's hand. While this is going on, the SCARECROW speaks.)

SCARECROW   So he told them. But we can't hear what his plan was, because that would spoil the rest of the play. (Looks across at the ANIMALS.)   It looks as though it's a good one, though, doesn't it? Well, we'll soon see.   (Turns in surprise as the STAGE MANAGER tiptoes on from the side.)   What's the matter now? We're in the middle of the play.

STAGE M.   (in piercing whisper)   What are we going to do about the lorry?

SCARECROW   The lorry? Oh yes, the lorry.   (To AUDIENCE.)

At this point, we were going to have a real lorry, but we couldn't get it in through the doors at the back. Now let me see, what shall we do?

(The SCENERY now move for the first time, and come D.S. to the SCARECROW and STAGE MANAGER.)

SCENERY 1   I don't mind being a lorry.

SCENERY 2   Neither do I. It's better than being a weeping willow tree, anyway.

SCENERY 1   I don't know. I'm so stiff after being a farmhouse that I can hardly straighten my shoulder – and my arm's gone to sleep.

SCENERY 3   But are there enough of us for a lorry?

SCARECROW   (rather impatiently)   Of course. You can manage somehow. Go on off and get yourselves sorted out.   (To STAGE MANAGER.)
You'd better go too, and get the Producer to help you.

(The SCENERY goes off.)

STAGE M.   (shaking his head as he follows them)   Oh, and it was such a lovely lorry –

SCARECROW   Interruptions! Interruptions! Now then, where were we? Oh yes.   (Takes up the tale again.)

(The ANIMALS have been watching with interest, but they now lie down and pretend to sleep as the SCARECROW speaks.)

That night, the animals all slept soundly, even though they were so worried about Percival, and the next morning –   (He turns to watch the action.)

(The ANIMALS wake, stretch and yawn.)

PERCIVAL   The lorry will be here soon to take me to London. I'm going to miss you all terribly.

GRANDFATHER T.   (to the SMALL TURKEY)   Over there, and keep a look-out.

(The SMALL TURKEY runs across the stage and watches the wings on the other side.)

Now then, Percival, buck up, there's a good fellow. Just you remember our plan, and you'll be back with us in no time.

A HEN   Oh, you're so clever, Grandfather Turkey.

PERCIVAL   I only hope the plan will work.

GRANDFATHER T.   Of course it will. I thought of it, didn't I?

(The SMALL TURKEY suddenly starts to jump up and down.)

SMALL TURKEY   (excitedly)   Hey, everybody – the lorry. It's coming.

GRANDFATHER T.   (putting his hand on PERCIVAL's shoulder)   Now then! Courage, Percival.

PERCIVAL   It's all right, Grandfather Turkey. I won't let you down. I'll be back, I promise.

(At this point, the LORRY enters. The LORRY DRIVER and his MATE stand upright in the front, with the SCENERY at the back – 1 and 3 at the back, and 2 in the middle. The SCENERY is bent over, holding onto each other's waists, and all shuffle on with small steps, while the DRIVER pretends to steer. The DRIVER mimes pulling on the handbrake, the LORRY slows down and stops D.S., and the DRIVER and his MATE get out on different sides. The ANIMALS are watching anxiously. The HEN gets out a handkerchief and pretends to cry into it.)

SCARECROW   As the animals watched, an enormous lorry rumbled into the farmyard and stopped.   (He watches it stop. This speech is punctuated with small pauses as he watches the ACTORS and waits for them to catch up with his words.)   The Lorry Driver and his Mate got out, went up the path to the farm door, and knocked on it loudly.

(They do so, in mime, and OLD MACDONALD comes out.)

LORRY DRIVER   (consulting a piece of paper)   Red Roofs Farm. Old Macdonald. One pig.

OLD M.   Ah, that'll be Percival. He's over there in the pigsty. I'll fetch him.

(OLD MACDONALD crosses to the ANIMALS, and shepherds PERCIVAL towards the LORRY. The following takes place as he goes.)

A HEN   (tearfully)   Oh Percival, you will take care of yourself in London, won't you?

PERCIVAL   Of course I will – and I'll be back in no time.

OLD M.   Now then, come along like a good pig, Percival.

SEVERAL ANIMALS   (waving)   Good luck – good luck –

OLD M.   Into the lorry you go.

(Assisted by the LORRY DRIVER and MATE, he lifts PERCIVAL onto the backs of the SCENERY – if PERCIVAL is not small enough to ride, he will have to stand among the SCENERY and wave as he walks out backwards.)

LORRY DRIVER   Right, mate. One pig it is.   (He and the MATE get back, each on their own side of the LORRY, and it moves off.)   Next stop, London.

GRANDFATHER T.   They're off. A big cheer for Percival, now. Come on, all of you, let's give him a good send-off –

ANIMALS   (waving and cheering)   Hooray! Goodbye, Percival! Good luck! Come back soon!

PERCIVAL   (waving from the back of the LORRY as it disappears into the wings)   Goodbye, my friends, goodbye –

(The LORRY disappears. The ANIMALS sit down tearfully. OLD MACDONALD watches the LORRY going along the road, looking thoughtful.)

A HEN   (applying handkerchief freely)   Oh, he's gone. Oh, I do hope he'll be all right –

GRANDFATHER T.   Now then, Henny! Pull yourself together. He'll be back.

A HEN   Yes, I suppose he will, but it's going to be awfully
                 lonely without him to sing to us.

                 (The others nod agreement, dry their tears, etc.
                 OLD MACDONALD shakes his head.)

OLD M.   You know something? I think I'm going to miss
                 Percival.   (He starts back towards the 'farm'.)

                 (The PRODUCER and STAGE MANAGER enter,
                 meeting OLD MACDONALD on the way. The
                 PRODUCER shakes him enthusiastically by the hand.)

PRODUCER   Splendid, splendid.   (To the others.)   You're
                 all doing marvellously. You know, I really think
                 we're managing quite well without the scenery.
                 (Looks approvingly towards the AUDIENCE.)   Not
                 one single rotten tomato. They must be enjoying it.

STAGE M.   (gloomily)   Perhaps they're saving the rotten
                 tomatoes till the end.   (Shakes head.)   When
                 I think of all that lovely scenery - that beautiful
                 chandelier -

                 (SCENERY 1 and SCENERY 2 enter.)

SCENERY 1   (briskly)   D'you want us to do any more, or can
                 we go now?

SCARECROW   Oh no, don't go. There are two more scenes yet.
                 (Looks at them.)   Where's John?

SCENERY 2   Oh, he had a puncture - I mean, he fell over. When
                 he was being the back wheel of the lorry. Here he
                 is.

                 (SCENERY 3 enters, rubbing his knee.)

STAGE M   (turning to ANIMALS)   What are you all sitting
                 there for? You're not supposed to be on now. This
                 is the hotel in London - isn't that right?   (To
                 PRODUCER.)

PRODUCER   (looking at a list)   That's it. Scene Three. A
                 Hotel in London. Enter Percival -

SCARECROW   Just a minute, we haven't got that far yet. What
                 about the scenery?

SCENERY 1	We're a hotel now, are we?
SCARECROW	(arranging them) Yes. You two can be the entrance doors (He places SCENERY 1 and 3 in the middle of the stage, at the back.) – and you can stand here (At left of doors.) and be a rubber plant.
SCENERY 2	Why must I be a rubber plant?
SCARECROW	Because that's what they have in the best hotels. (Turns to AUDIENCE.) Of course, our scenery was really much nicer than this. We had the walls papered with red and gold, and swing doors, of course, and a beautiful staircase curving up at the side, with a deep red carpet. Then we had a desk here for the Manager – (Turns to PRODUCER.) Where is he, by the way? I hope he knows he's on in this scene.
PRODUCER	(shouting into wings) Scene Three! Actors on stage!
	(The HOTEL MANAGER hurries on, adjusting his tie. He is in semi-formal dress.)
HOTEL M.	Here I am. There's only me. I'm not late, am I?
PRODUCER	Just get behind the desk, ready for Percival's entrance –
HOTEL M.	(anxiously) There isn't a desk.
PRODUCER	(exasperated) Well, pretend there is. (Looks round.) Now, I think we're all ready –
STAGE M.	No! No! No! Get these animals out of here – come on, shoo! Shoo!
	(The ANIMALS, who have been watching with interest, get up reluctantly, and file off the stage.)
GRANDFATHER T.	Oh, all right. We're going.
	(Exeunt ANIMALS, and the STAGE MANAGER with them.)
PRODUCER	(looking round again) Okay then, Scarecrow. Off you go. (He goes out quietly.)

SCARECROW
(back in his corner)   Later that day, the lorry arrived in London, and Percival was taken to the best hotel –   (Turns to watch the action.)

(PERCIVAL comes in through the 'doors' and the HOTEL MANAGER goes forward to greet him.)

HOTEL M.
Mr Percival Pig, I believe? May I welcome you to our hotel, sir?   (They shake hands.)
Mr Potter informed me that you would be arriving.

PERCIVAL
Is Mr Potter here?

HOTEL M.
No, but he will be arriving shortly –

(HIRAM enters through the 'doors'.)

Oh, here he is. Good afternoon, sir, I'll leave you two gentlemen alone together.   (He bows and exits.)

HIRAM
(slapping PERCIVAL on the shoulder)   Splendid to see you, old chap. Well, I've made all the arrangements. You are to sing tonight. Why, by this time tomorrow, you'll be famous.

(They hold this pose, then look round in surprise as the STAGE MANAGER hurries on.)

(in his ordinary voice)   Oh – oh! Next scene. We'd better go and change.

PERCIVAL
I hope I can squeeze into that costume – it's a bit on the small side.

(They go off.)

STAGE M.
(wringing hands anxiously)   Oh dear, oh dear. Here we are at the theatre scene already, and no chandelier. What are we going to do?

SCENERY 2
Is that the end of the hotel bit, then? Didn't take long, did it?

STAGE M.
(busily improvising a chandelier)   Perhaps if one of you could swing down from the roof, holding a torch –

SCARECROW
(joining them)   You've simply got to face it,

there is no chandelier, and there isn't going to be
one, either.   (Turns to AUDIENCE.)   We
had a lovely one with our scenery, you know. This
next scene takes place in the theatre, you see. We
had red plush seats for the audience on this side
(Points.)   and a blue velvet stage curtain over
there   (Points.)   and in the middle, high
up –

STAGE M   The chandelier! Sparkling like a million diamonds
as the audience gathered in their seats –

SCENERY 2   (practically)   Well, I can tell you one thing –
I'm not being a chandelier.

SCENERY 1   Neither am I. It's far too risky.

SCENERY 3   And I don't fancy being a red plush seat, either.

OTHERS   (in agreement)   No, nor me.

SCARECROW   (to AUDIENCE)   You see our difficulties? Wait –
(Stares out into the AUDIENCE.)   Are my eyes
deceiving me? No – there are two empty seats out
there. How very fortunate.   (To SCENERY 2.)
Go and tell the Producer we're ready to carry on.

(SCENERY 2 goes off, and comes back with the
PRODUCER, while the SCARECROW speaks to the
rest of the SCENERY.)

(to SCENERY)   Now then. This scene is
Percival's dressing room, back-stage at the theatre.
You two   (Arranges them.)   can be his
make-up table, with greasepaints and things, you
know, and lights all round the mirror – and you
(To SCENERY 2.)   can be his – er, his –

SCENERY 2   (resigned)   I suppose I'll have to be a potted
plant again.

SCARECROW   Yes, that's right. You can be a Busy Lizzie, for a
change. Stand over there.   (To PRODUCER.)
Okay for the next scene?

PRODUCER   (shouting)   Scene Four. Actors on stage.

STAGE M.   (suddenly realising)   But they're not on stage

	this time – they have to come on –
PRODUCER	Oh yes. How silly of me. Well, off you go, Scarecrow.
	(Exit all except SCARECROW and SCENERY. The SCARECROW comes back to his corner.)
SCARECROW	(taking up the story) That night, the audience gathered in the theatre. All the ladies were in evening dress, and all the gentlemen wore bow ties. Everybody was very excited. They could hardly wait to hear the wonderful voice of Percival, the Performing Pig – (He turns to watch the action.)
	(Enter the THEATRE MANAGER, with LORD POSH and LADY POSH. All in full evening dress, including fan, tiara, etc.)
THEATRE M.	I'm so glad you were able to be with us tonight, Lord Posh and Lady Posh. If you'll just follow me, I'll show you to your seats. (He leads the way down off the stage to two empty seats in the front row. The following is spoken as they walk to their seats.)
LADY POSH	This pig has a fantastic voice, so I hear, Mr Manager.
THEATRE M.	It's magnificent, madame. I've never heard one like it – never in my whole career as a Theatre Manager.
LORD POSH	What's he going to sing – pop songs?
THEATRE M.	Oh no, Lord Posh. We're starting with some famous songs from operas, and then, as a finale, Percival is going to sing a duet with himself.
LADY POSH	That should be very interesting.
THEATRE M.	It's quite unique, madame, I can assure you, quite unique. And now, I must hurry back-stage. The curtain will be rising in a few moments. (Bows and hurries back onto the stage and off into the wings.)
	(LORD and LADY POSH sit unobtrusively. Meanwhile, the SCARECROW speaks.)
SCARECROW	But in Percival's dressing room behind the stage,

Mr Potter was nearly chewing his cigar with rage.
(Turns back to watch the action.)

(PERCIVAL, dressed in some sort of theatrical
costume, walks on calmly. HIRAM hurries after
him, waving his cigar frantically.)

HIRAM

(shouting)   What's all this? What's all this?
How dare you tell me you won't sing tonight –

PERCIVAL

(calmly)   I didn't say I won't. I said I can't.
That's a different thing altogether. Listen to this –
(He mimes the singing of a note.)

(HIRAM screws up his face and puts his hands over
his ears in horror. SCARECROW speaks the
commentary.)

SCARECROW

And he sang a note which didn't sound lovely at all.
In fact, it sounded exactly like the sort of noise a
pig usually makes.

PERCIVAL

You see, my voice has gone. The air in London is
so dirty – not a bit like the fresh, clean air on my
farm – and my voice has altered.

HIRAM

(bawling)   Altered, has it? We'll soon see about
that.   (Starts to dash off, but bumps into
THEATRE MANAGER.)

THEATRE M.

Why, Mr Potter, where are you going? The curtain's
due to rise at any moment.

HIRAM

(shouting as he rushes off)   Fetch doctors –
Doctor Wheezum – Doctor Sneezum – where are they?

THEATRE M.

(to PERCIVAL)   Oh dear, oh dear. Has something
gone wrong?

PERCIVAL

(mysteriously)   We'll soon see.   (Gives
thumbs-up sign unobtrusively to AUDIENCE.)

(Enter HIRAM with three DOCTORS, in a row. They
are dressed in top hats and formal clothes, with
spectacles, and should look as alike as possible.
They carry large bottles marked 'syrup', 'honey' and
'tonic'.)

HIRAM

(to PERCIVAL)   Doctor Wheezum – Doctor

Sneezum – Doctor Tonic. May I introduce you
gentlemen to Percival, the Performing Pig.

THEATRE M.   (anxiously)   But Mr Potter, what is all this?

HIRAM   The curtain due to go up at any moment – at any
                moment – and he has the nerve to tell me he's lost
                his voice.

PERCIVAL   I didn't say that at all. I just said – oh well, listen
                for yourselves –   (He mimes a note again.)

                (Everybody, including the SCARECROW, expresses
                horror.)

THEATRE M.   Oh dear, oh dear. To think that this should have
                happened in my theatre –

HIRAM   (to DOCTORS)   Well, what are you standing
                there for? Do something!

                (The DOCTORS line up in front of PERCIVAL.)

WHEEZUM   Open wide please.

                (PERCIVAL does so.)

SNEEZUM   Wider.

TONIC   Much wider.

WHEEZUM   Say 'Ah'.

PERCIVAL   (strangled gasp)   Aaaah!

SNEEZUM   (lifting a finger significantly)   Ah!

TONIC   Ahh – hah!

HIRAM   (impatiently)   Well?

WHEEZUM   (getting out enormous spoon)   My soothing syrup
                should do the trick.

SNEEZUM   (also getting out spoon)   A dose of my honey,
                and he'll be as good as new.

TONIC   (also with spoon)   What he needs is a tonic.
                (Waves bottle.)

                (They put their heads together briefly.)

WHEEZUM   So in order to make quite sure he gets his voice back –

SNEEZUM	We've decided to give him a dose of everything –
TONIC	Just to be on the safe side.
HIRAM	(impatiently) Well, hurry up and get on with it.
	(The DOCTORS line up, each pours a 'dose' from their bottle onto the spoon, and PERCIVAL goes along the line, pretending to swallow each.)
WHEEZUM	(as PERCIVAL drinks) Syrup –
SNEEZUM	(as PERCIVAL drinks) Honey –
TONIC	(as PERCIVAL drinks) Tonic –
ALL TOGETHER	We now pronounce him cured.
HIRAM	Thank goodness for that. (To THEATRE MANAGER.) Get out there and ring up the curtain – we're late already –
THEATRE M.	(nervously) Wouldn't it be better to just check first – I mean, just to make sure Percival's really got his voice back?
HIRAM	Oh all right. Sing us a note, old chap.
	(PERCIVAL mimes clearing throat, patting chest, etc., and opens his mouth just as the SCARECROW finishes speaking.)
SCARECROW	So Percival did. And can you guess what he sounded like?
	(As PERCIVAL opens his mouth, the others screw up their faces and clap their hands over their ears.)
HIRAM	What? What? (To DOCTORS.) I thought you said you'd cured him.
DOCTORS	(hurriedly backing towards the wings) Just a small oversight – unforseen circumstances – very rare case – (They scurry off the stage.)
PERCIVAL	(to HIRAM) It's not their fault. I told you – it's the air here in London. I just can't sing when I'm away from home.
HIRAM	(gloomily) Oh well – I know when I'm beaten.

	(To THEATRE MANAGER.) You'd better go and tell the audience. Give them their money back –
THEATRE M.	(leaving the stage) Oh dear, oh dear, what a catastrophe!
HIRAM	(to PERCIVAL) And what am I going to do with you? A pig's no use to me unless it can do something.
PERCIVAL	Well, couldn't you sell me back to Old Macdonald?
HIRAM	(brightening up) That's an idea. I'll go and telephone him right away. (He hurries off.)
PERCIVAL	(sharing triumph with AUDIENCE) Good old Grandfather Turkey. It worked like a charm, didn't it? This time tomorrow, I'll be back home on the farm.
	(PRODUCER and STAGE MANAGER hurry on.)
PRODUCER	A brilliant performance, absolutely brilliant.
SCENERY 2	Have we finished now?
STAGE M.	No, not quite. There's just one more scene.
SCENERY 1	Where we take our bows, you mean?
SCENERY 3	That's the part I like best. (To ACTORS in the wings.) Hey, come on, everybody, it's the scene where we take our bows.
GRANDFATHER T.	(poking his head on stage) Is it?
A HEN	(doing the same) Is it?
STAGE M.	(waving them off) No, not yet. We've got to have Percival going home in the lorry first.
SCENERY 2	Not a lorry again.
SCENERY 1	(leading the way off) I'm going to claim a petrol allowance for this.
PRODUCER	Where's the Lorry Driver? Get him, somebody. Everybody off – Right, ready, Scarecrow?
	(All leave the stage as the SCARECROW takes up the tale.)

SCARECROW   There's really not much more to tell.

(As the SCARECROW speaks, the LORRY, with
PERCIVAL riding on the back, passes across the back
of the stage, stopping in the centre if required, for
as long as is necessary.)

Old Macdonald agreed to have Percival back again,
and the next day, the lorry arrived to take him home
to the farm. And do you know what? As soon as the
lorry got outside London, a beautiful song could be
heard.

(PERCIVAL mimes singing.)

It was Percival. You didn't think he'd really lost
his voice, did you? And he sang all the way home.

(Exit LORRY, with PERCIVAL waving as it disappears.
The SCARECROW bows, and goes U.C. to join the
others. All take bows together. If required, the end
of 'Old Macdonald had a farm' can be played as the
play finishes and the curtain falls.)

CURTAIN

Printed in Great Britain by Latimer Trend & Company Ltd, Plymouth